w(In Our Own)rds

Promoting insight and understanding of self harm

Foreword

I first met Caroline Roe when I was filming a BBC documentary for their Head Room series, rather challengingly called Self Harm; A World Of Pain back in 2008. In fact, challenging was the buzz word for the journey I went on for the programme to try and understand an issue which is so prevalent and yet so hidden and misunderstood. I had had some experience of the issues and complexities around SH, due to my long standing involvement with the campaigning East London based organisation, Newham Asian Women's project, whose patron I've been for ten years. They were amongst the first group to identify the escalating incidence of SH amongst Asian women and respond incredibly quickly to the needs of their users who were self harming, with support groups, awareness training and pioneering research. So I wasn't starting from a complete position of ignorance, but it was only when we began filming that I realised how little I truly knew. And then I met Caroline...

Our research team brought her in to advise, comment and generally hold my hand during a session we held at a London school, where we hoped to have an honest discussion with a group of young people about their experience and awareness of Self Harm. It had been incredibly difficult finding any school who would allow us in to even broach what they regarded as an explosive, emotive subject and I was nervous. Caroline had been identified as someone who had an impressive track record in talking to young people about SH, her organisation Harmless was doing sterling work in various schools and colleges and most importantly, she seemed to be someone whom people trusted, that was obvious from her web site and testimonials. It was only when I saw her in action that I realised how very good she was; her sensitivity, her intelligence, her non judgemental approach, above all her openess and humour got the room talking, the students had a lot to say and somehow, Caroline had created the space for them to say it. That takes a special kind of skill.

Since the programme aired, I've had many people contacting me for advice, some on a confidential basis, and I have recommended all of them to Harmless. And all of them got in contact later to sing Harmless' praises, many of them parents frantic with worry about a beloved child, who came away from Harmless feeling less alone, more supported, and most importantly, with hope that a painful situation might in time, with care and support, be resolved.

Harmless is amazing, and I think, so is this book. Maybe enjoy isn't the right word, but I hope you come away from it feeling enlightened, surprised and moved by the contributions in these pages. So many stories, and the more we can share, the more we can know.

Meera Syal.

Introduction

"Strength does not come from physical capacity,
it comes from an indomitable will"
Gandhi

Monday night, 8.30pm in a large office and four people are stood around eighty spread out pages of what has become this book in your hands. Exchanging smiles and the occasional squeal of excitement, we cannot quite believe that before us is something that is so special not just to us, but to every single person who will read it. It has been months of work and now we have a chance to deliver a message, one of hope, one of determination, one to share with you.

'Self harm' is a term that describes when a person deliberately hurts themselves. It is a coping strategy that sometimes helps people manage emotional stress. It can affect anyone whatever their age, ethnic background or sexual orientations. In some situations it doesn't just affect the individual's who are suffering, but their family, friends and supporters too.

In Our Own Words is a book which shares the experiences of self harm from those who may be suffering, their friends, their families and even the professionals who have worked with individuals and their struggles. It has been put together to draw insight and inspiration not just for those who have experienced self harm, but also to share with those who want to understand self harm and the issues surrounding the reasons why someone may do so. The book aims to promote understanding and contains words and images generated by people whose lives have been touched by self harm - some of these people just wanting to share positive words for those who may need it.

This has been a year-long project for a team who have formed the editorial group for this book. Every member of the group has their own stories and experiences connected to self harm and have drawn strength from this project, shaping the journey of the book as they progressed. The book set out with the original aims to be useful and inspiring and ready to challenge the stigmas and stereotypes that come with the words self harm. We also wanted to reach out to others; to help those suffering realise they are not alone and that support is out there as and when they need it.

When we advertised for submissions, we did not expect the overwhelming amount of response we received. When we say response, we don't just mean the huge amount of submissions, but the support in words of others, people from all over the world who wanted to encourage the project and were looking forward to seeing the final product. As for the selection process, it wasn't easy to make the decisions we made but we are pleased with the pieces we have chosen. Each piece in this book communicates the issues, feelings and struggles relating to self harm as well as sharing the understanding and compassion. They reveal the real people behind the stigmas, and it is their courage and strength alone which has brought this book together.

The people who have contributed to this book come from all walks of life. They are men, women, young people, old people, parents, children, siblings, doctors, professionals, sufferers, partners and friends. The submissions come from all over the world as far as India to the USA and as local as Nottingham to Derby. The spectrum of backgrounds of each person proves that beyond the stereotypes lives an individual.

We hope that the pages this book contains will offer you a new perspective on self harm. Here we give you our collection of stories, photographs, poems and pictures - the words of individuals.

Special thanks to Open Up Media for funding the book, Time To change, deviantArt, Recover Your Life, MIND and Lorna for her design work.

Most importantly thank you to everyone who has supported, encouraged and contributed to this project, for without you we wouldn't have achieved this.

Finally, thank you to you, for picking up this book.

The Editorial Group

Caroline Roe

Caroline is 30 and one of the founding members and a Director of Harmless, and initiated the creation of this book. She has since been a passionate member of the editorial group, alongside her daily role in the management of the overall project. Caroline has a long history of mental health problems and self harm, some of which are documented in these pages. Despite these experiences, she has recovered from her difficulties and spends her time working to promote health and hope for others. This book is a labour of love – it brings together the spirit and passion of hope that Caroline believes faithfully in, and the beauty of writing and art.

Caroline is moved by the pieces in this book, and is so proud to see this project come to fruition.

Rebecca Turney

Rebecca, 25, holds a degree in Creative Writing and Theatre and works part time as a drama teacher. She is determined to give a voice to people who self harm as well as show others the people behind the stigmas. Her own experience in self harm is personal mostly through social struggles at school and university. She has overcome these issues from the support and strength of friends, family and her partner Joseph. In her spare time she writes, enjoys football and the theatre.

Heather Williams

Heather, 24, struggled with self harm for several years and has now overcome her battle. She first came into contact with members of the Harmless Team looking for support and is now in a position where she can offer the same help to others as a volunteer and a Director, and a member of the editorial group. At first Heather felt daunted by the task of creating this book, but now feels that has been an amazing experience watching it take shape. She is both excited and proud of what has been achieved.

Rachel Anderson

Rachel is 32 and works in a support capacity within Education. Personal experience of self harm led to her interest and involvement with Harmless and the In Our Own Words Book project. The book seemed like an excellent way to reach out to others who self harm and she was thrilled when she was asked to be involved. Rachel first used self-harm to help her cope when she was in her early teens and this continued to varying degrees for around 16 years. Throughout this time Rachel developed a personal understanding of the stigma and shame related to self harm and mental health.

She hopes that her involvement with the book will help to break down barriers for people and reduce the isolation they may feel. On a personal level it has helped her to feel less shame and is an achievement she can be proud of.

Lorna Gillam

Lorna Gillam, 25, is the designer for this book. She became involved with the Harmless project because of her own experiences, and a desire to help and reach out to others. She has been responsible for the layout and design of this book, and feels that the experiences shared in these pages will help people realise that they are not alone and will raise awareness of self harm. She believes that this book gives a positive message that there is hope for recovery and hopes that this book will go a long way in challenging attitudes about self harm.

Also thanks to...

Three other members, Hannah Freebury, James Moran and Garry Trevatt were also members of the editorial group. Their personal experiences of self harm motivated them to engage in this project, and try to raise awareness, challenge stigma, and reduce isolation for people who are still struggling. Their contributions have helped to make this project happen.

THIS IS A SCAR.

22nd of September, 2002.

The doctor and her driver just dropped me outside A & E. I am crying, shaking and I feel very much alone. I drop my keys and fumble for them on the ground whilst balancing my heavy rucksack on my shoulder. I'm clutching to my letter – the letter that the GP had just handed me and told me to take to the hospital.

When I report to the reception desk, they are expecting me. I am told to wait with the other unfortunate souls that find themselves here at this time of night. The waiting area is full, as people hold their heads and arms in pain. I have nothing to clutch, except my heart that feels as though it is bleeding out all the pain in my body. Instead I wrap my arms around my bag and weep into it quietly.

I know people look at me. I withdraw inside myself and try to become smaller, so no one can see me. I am invisible in my mind; as is my pain.

A friendly looking nurse calls my name and I stop being invisible. I stand and follow her to another waiting area. Here, the patients sit in rows, all facing me. I am told to take a seat but I cannot move. The only available seat is right at the back and a sea of faces to go with it. Five behind five behind five pairs of staring eyes. My heart is now pounding; racing. My legs shuffle and I prepare to run. Instead, I turn to the nurse terrified and burst into tears. Everyone is staring at me, but I cannot stop. I put my hands to my face to try and hide my distress, but I cannot hide. It's too big to hide anymore.

The nurse kindly guides me to a cubicle and draws the curtain and I am left alone. I cry.

They tell me that the doctor won't be long; time both stands still and races past me. I am lost to it. I don't belong in this world. I don't breathe the same air as other people. I don't think the same way. There is no place for me.

Eventually the doctor arrives with nurses and they look at my wounds which are all throbbing and sore now. They poke around and pinch the cuts together, and then tell me that I need to be stitched. I am terrified. I describe to them the situation I find myself in and I tell of the blackness, the panic, the fear.

I seem to have reduced myself to a grain of sand, sitting right in the middle of my head. My vision becomes tunnelled and dark, the sounds are muffled and distant as I try so hard to protect myself from the moment I find myself in. I KNOW that I am answering their questions, but it doesn't feel like me – it is the me that I call upon when I cannot cope. The me that gives a voice to the voiceless.

I can hear myself telling them that I don't know how else to cope, but they don't understand. They must think that I am wasting their time and I feel so ashamed. I am desperate for someone to hear me, just to hear how it is that I am feeling. I can feel it mounting up inside of me and then it gets unbearable so I take it out on myself. It is only then in that brief moment that all the emotion gets washed away. But then, afterwards, I am left with this; with scars and pain, humiliation and shame.

I sit here whilst they sew my legs back together like a patchwork quilt. I look at what I have done to myself and I promise myself, like every other time, I will never do this again – that this time I will find a new way of coping. I don't know how, but I will.

But it will happen again, wont it? Because it always does. It hurts so badly, and I try to wish it all away, but I know that I must deserve this.

Later:

I'm listening to the weather forecast on the radio: highs of 18°c, the weather outside is dull, damp and miserable. The weather inside is worse.

Let me describe the room; a square, 12' square. The walls are a smoke-tinged yellow, like the walls of a neglected public house. There are five high-backed PVC chairs that look as if they have been slashed and cut into. The foam spills out of their gouges. There is a fan, twisting and turning its gnarled head in protest, forcing the heavy smoke from one side of the room to the other.

I could lose myself in here for good, amidst the floral curtains and the pasty walls, the echoed footsteps and voices in hallways. Nothing matters in here; not the way I look, or the way I dress, or whether I wash my hair. This is not me. I should not be here.

Someone sings out from the radio: "oh baby, come on... I need you to show me how to start living my life..." Maybe I am hearing words being called to me from outside these walls. I need someone to show me how to start living my life. I need someone to teach me how to cope, right from the start. I am a child again. I am as I was as a child: without guidance. This is my way of coping, this is my way and this is my best.

This is not good enough.

22nd September, 2009.

This was written at the depth of a despairing time, when the only thing that seemed to surround me was a world that didn't understand my struggle. I was the girl that hurt herself so badly that the doctors just hadn't the patience to keep 'fixing me', nor the care for why it was happening. I was the girl that spent hours crying quietly to herself, wishing someone would notice and help. I didn't need much, but what I really needed was a touch of human compassion.

Instead I was the girl that mental health services labelled as 'attention-seeking', the girl that they said couldn't be helped and the girl that they wrote off as an 'expected suicide'. Today I am a Director of Harmless and one of its co-founders. After years of suffering, when human compassion was eventually offered to me I turned the corner.

Seven years on I now spend every day working to help others the way that they helped me; people who face similar experiences of distress and despair to get the help, the compassion and the support that was lacking in my own struggles. I am precisely the reason why Harmless needs to exist, why we have to listen to the voiceless and believe beyond everything, that people can triumph over their pain. Having hope is such a difficult thing when the world seems bleak, so I, and Harmless, hope you (after reading this) can above all else, remain hopeful for change. Distress is subjective, and whatever has driven someone to self harm, whether it is a bad day at work or abuse, it matters. Give people the chance to define their selves and to describe their struggles in their own words. Give people the space where it is ok to just be.

Self harm and despair can be overcome. If we work hard enough, if we help hard enough – recovery happens.

Some of the individuals that helped me to save my life have also contributed to this book.

Caroline Roe

Becky and I met about four years ago online in a chat room. It was full of teenage girls like us, but still we found each other. It began with small talk, but soon became something deeper. We became friends and started to talk on a daily basis. A few months after our first "Hello" I found out just how important she had become to me. We lost our access to the Internet for a few days and I was seriously going crazy. All my thoughts revolved around Becky and the things I wanted to tell her. She got a real long e-mail when I was able to go online again. It was then that I realised she had become my best and closest friend.

Naturally, my parents started to worry. The Internet is suspicious to them, and so is everyone you get to meet there. When Becky said her parents were concerned, too, we set up a meeting. She and her family took on the five hour car ride to stay with my family for a weekend. Miraculously our parents got along fine and mine liked Becky just as much as hers liked me. Moreover it was great to be able to really talk to my best friend – so much better than chatting online. After the weekend our parents agreed to let us meet once a month. I would visit her and she would visit me in return.

Years passed, but the bond between us stayed the same. The time came when we were able to drive ourselves to visit the other, but we stuck to the monthly meetings. We still had the Internet and the occasional phone call and that was enough, I thought. We were so used to it.

Then one day Becky didn't turn up online all day. That might not sound bad to you, but it had never happened before, so I started to worry. At first I thought that

Snapshots

Sarah Pohl

maybe something was wrong with their Internet connection or telephone line. After two days of not hearing anything from her, I took up the phone and called. It was her mother who answered and told me what had happened. I passed the phone on to my dad, packed a few things and drove the five hour trip in four and a half. Still, I didn't make it in time to see her, so I slept at her parent's house to accompany them to the clinic the next day.

I didn't sleep much that night, and just like before alone in my car I wondered how it could have come to this. I had seen her in T-shirts and shorts so often, saw her smile and laugh and she was happy. I never noticed any scars, neither on the outside nor on the inside. Nevertheless she had had to be institutionalised for seriously hurting herself. She had this problem for years, they say.

When I stood before her that day at the clinic, she knew exactly what I thought and felt. She put her hand onto my cheek and looked deep into my tear-filled eyes. Her words are carved into my heart forever:

"Honey," she said, "the Internet is nothing. What we say there doesn't mean a thing. A whole human character doesn't fit on the screen. And we only met once a month. 36 days out of 365. Those were snapshots, nothing more. I always smile for the camera. It's easy to pretend for such a short time. It's not your fault you didn't know, it was my choice."

Becky gets help at the clinic, she is recovering and we talk a lot; honest talk this time. My view of the world was shattered that day; I guess it was only a snapshot.

Snapshots

Photograph by Caroline Roe

How do I tell my Story?

Chris Kenda

There is a frightened child
Trapped in this woman's head
The cuts and scars I have
Are words never said

My past was filled with pain
I was a worthless child
The only comfort I had
Was a secret deep inside

My cutting was my comfort
The bleeding, my release
Of all the fear and torment
I endure without any peace

My days became much darker
The pain too much to bear
So I turned to tablets
Without any thought or care

From one to two, to many
Eventually to more with drink
My cutting was not helping
It brought me to the brink

In calmness and in quiet
To save me, a mad dash
The family all in uproar
The situation, a car crash

What followed was a nightmare
Of recrimination and anger
How could I be so cruel?
Why did I put myself in danger?

The physical quickly healed
Emotions took lots more time
But still I was in denial
I hadn't committed any crime?

So, on and on I persevered
Resorting to my old ways
Always to feel sad and lonely
I believed till the end of days

The chaos still persisted
But I learned to ignore it
Until once more it returned
To overwhelm and erupt

Once more into the service
Of A & E, and Mental Health
But instead of rejection
There was sincere help

The staff were there to help me
They listened and empathised
They understood all my fears
And helped me realise

That cuts and pills were words
That I did not know or say
They helped me learn a language
To express myself each day

It was no individual
But a mighty team
Who comfort and support me
And challenge my beliefs

I always strive to be perfect
To please everyone around
But by caring for myself
There are many things I found

I was blameless for my Past
I was just a small child
How could I cope with feelings?
With no one by my side

The Past is forgone history
The Future is still to arrive
The Present my family and life
now I know, I really can survive

My life is far from perfect
There's still challenges every day
But with love, support and friendship
I can cope with what comes my way

I have grown so used to my scars that I am hardly aware of them now. Sometimes though, someone will say, "What happened to your arm?" Then I have to decide whether to tell them about the self-harm or to bluff it out and say I had a terrible accident. The latter is hardly believable given the nature of the scars and it's hard to casually change the subject as though the question was unimportant.

The question certainly isn't of no consequence since it takes me back to a time when I was so tormented that I tore at myself like a caged animal. The voices I heard told me to cut myself till the blood ran - I believed the wounds to be a protection against suicide but they were also a way of putting the pain on the outside of me rather than hold it inside. At the hospital, when I needed stitching, they were often less than sympathetic. I was a 'DSH' - a case of deliberate self-harm - and the nurses had no time for a woman who inflicted injury on herself. Perhaps though, they should have tried to understand.

It was many years ago now, and my life has changed. I channelled the hurt into creative work, making the destructive constructive. Creating images that expressed my feelings about the voices and the pain and writing words that fell like drops of blood from my pen. It is possible to turn the pain into creative expression - it really is. Paint it, write it, sing it out loud or dance it if you can. Just find your own way to express the tangled hurt inside.

As I have progressed and the years have passed, my art has moved on and I can now work creatively in other ways. I still have my dark side and when those feelings become too great, I have my images and words to reflect my feelings. Yes, I sometimes feel driven to harm myself but, for the most part, I don't need to anymore.

Overload

Alison Philbey

Busy body, busy mind,
Keep the juices flowing round.
Adrenaline in plenty rushes,
Though not so much emotion gushes.

Busy eyes, busy ears,
Focus thoughts away from fears.
From one task to another glide
So not into the abyss I'll slide.

Now the action's stopped a while
Lost the frenzy, lost the smile.
All other human presence gone,
Emotions say, "You're all alone"!

Alone in office, car or house -
Alone in all the Universe.
Terror... desperation... Hell
Take over from sight, hearing, smell.

So bang the head or bite the hand,
Pull the hair or fist the land.
P A I N... and then the pulse... slows... down;
A few deep breaths to smooth the frown;
Restore the roles of pro and clown.

Untitled

My sense of shame and desperate isolation was overwhelming. I was in hospital; in a busy A & E department, and I'd cut myself – badly.

This wasn't the first time; I'd lost count of all the previous episodes. Arguably, I'd been hurting myself since I was a very small child, when I would scratch and bite myself impulsively in response to feelings which I could neither describe nor understand. Now I was 22, under pressure; working towards the finals of a teaching degree, in the midst of a relationship crisis and slowly spiralling into depression.

I didn't know – I hadn't learnt how to express myself. Home hadn't been a place to talk about things. I'd experienced anger as something terrifying that involved shouting and hitting. Problems and feelings were not shared and so I learned to cry alone. The betrayal of my fiancé broke me inside and I wanted to give up – it was too hard and too painful.

Those un-named and unexpressed emotions were like a restrained animal which I fought to control. I was losing strength, and the smallest, most unexpected thing had the power to unleash the torrent of anger, frustration and devastation that was locked inside.

I shocked myself the first time I did it; not the biting or scratching, but the more serious injury. Almost immediately, I was no longer aware of the feelings and tension, as I experienced an incredible sense of calm and relief. I watched, it had a kind of 'hypnotic' effect. I had no idea what was happening and no understanding of why I had chosen this bizarre method of making myself 'feel better.'

I feared I must be mad. I was terrified that if anyone knew, I would be sent away and locked up. This was not rational behaviour.

I hid the evidence by wearing long sleeves to cover the bandages. It was my secret; my shameful secret, but something I needed to do in order to tolerate those awful feelings. I wanted to talk to someone, but I was too scared.

I was in hospital, in a cubicle on my own, being faced with a hostile nurse and a 'silent doctor.' I'd hurt myself in the toilets at the University when revision got too much, but I unintentionally went too far. I wasn't calm, I was panicking - the damage I'd done was dangerous. I grabbed my things and endeavoured to cycle home, but I fell off the bike into the road and the ambulance was called.

I was so ashamed and exposed sitting in that white, clinical cubicle. My secret was out and I awaited my fate. I sat there for a long time, wondering where I'd be locked up.

At this point, I had no idea that any other person hurt themselves as I did. I thought the medical staff would be shocked, but they seemed more angry and frustrated with me. I was called a 'silly girl', and stitched up by a nurse who neither spoke nor gave me eye contact. I felt as if I was being punished for being distressed. The lack of interaction reminded me of the 'silent treatment' I received as a child when I'd been naughty. I was stitched up and told to go home.

The self harm continued and escalated. I avoided hospital whenever possible but sometimes the injuries necessitated a return to the hated A&E. The treatment I received only served to reinforce my firmly established low opinion of myself. It was a horrible, seemingly endless cycle in which I was becoming totally trapped.

Amazingly I graduated, but was then immediately thrust into the bewildering world of 'Mental Health Services,' which was to be my life for the next 17 years.

I became a 'service user,' client, patient - with the labels: 'depressed,' 'Borderline Personality disorder,' 'Eating disordered' and chronic self-harmer; taking away any sense of the person I was before.

I hated myself and my life; I had no future.

Maybe I hadn't completely lost hope, because however hard it became I would still attend my therapy - deep down, I hoped it would help. The internal battle was pulling me apart inside though; I still held tightly to the 'security' of self harm, because it worked; it helped alleviate those raging emotions that I could not control. My life deteriorated into a chaotic mix of self harm/hospital admissions/A&E visits and long periods of complete withdrawal from the outside world. I lost any sense of who I was because I had allowed myself to be taken over by the identity of a 'mental health service user' and for a long time I couldn't imagine I would ever be anything else.

One of the serious (planned) attempts on my life had a massive impact on me. As I lay in my bed in the cardiac mobilisation ward after the overdose, I felt ashamed and confused. I didn't really want to die - I just couldn't find a way of living. I'd been simply enduring an 'existence' for a long time and I'd had enough.

In the midst of the darkest time where I could see no way forward, hope came through two people who were like parents to me. I was overwhelmed by their support and care; they made me feel secure and protected, possibly for the first time in my life.

There were many years of therapy that were sadly unproductive; mainly because no one was prepared to accept that I self harmed. Any treatment came to a premature end, because self harm was deemed unacceptable and so further offers of therapy were conditional on no self harm. The fact was that I needed help to address the cutting in order to safely address the painful underlying issues that caused me to do it in the first place! In the opinion of the Psychiatrist, I was 'untreatable' and so discharged from all services, sent home and told to get a job. My despair and sense of utter hopelessness led to another suicide attempt.

A new GP and a move back to my home town brought with it a tiny spark of renewed hope.

I was told about a new therapy called 'DBT' (Dialectical Behaviour Therapy). It sounded a bit weird and complicated, but what I did know was that its main focus was on reducing/eliminating self harming behaviours and learning other ways to cope with difficult emotions. That was enough for me to find out more, and with a little persuasion, go for an assessment and get accepted on the programme.

I was unprepared for having to talk about every single self harming episode in great detail. I was required to examine my thoughts, feelings and 'chain of events' preceding and following, every time I cut myself. This was exposure to the limit, but I persevered.

I began to understand myself more and identify those emotions, which for so long, had been avoided by self harm. It was intense and painful, but I was determined to carry on; albeit with a degree of ambivalence at the prospect of a life without my tried and tested coping mechanism; if indeed, such a life could ever be possible for me.

I started to read more and discovered that there was a wealth of literature out there, which could help and inform me and certainly make me aware that I was not 'the only one.' Each time I 'slipped up' and hurt myself again; I could go back and talk about it. Many times I felt a complete failure and wondered if I could keep holding on to that hope that things could be better. It was proving to be the hardest challenge of my life so far. My circle of support was strong, but remained small, because I was vulnerable. I'd lost my closest friend by telling her how I 'coped' and it felt too risky to expose myself to further potential rejection.

DBT required me to talk about things that I'd never previously spoken of. I cried a lot and it hurt so much inside that I couldn't imagine that I'd recover. The unfamiliar experience of pouring out my emotions left me feeling raw and exhausted. My whole system of controlling my emotions was being dismantled and it was very frightening. My friends never gave up on me, they were kind and consistently supportive. Sometimes they pointed things out to me that were difficult to hear, but I respected and trusted them.

Over time, the therapy offered other ways to manage my feelings, and gradually the frequency and severity of the self harm decreased. It was never easy and the pull towards the old way remained strong when things were really hard.

DBT was ten years ago. I'm now 41 and doing paid work for the first time in 17 years. For the last ten years, what I have done is to start to talk about self harm more widely – to educate people, increase their understanding and challenge the stigma which sadly still exists. From somewhere, I've found my voice to speak; at conferences, workshops, user and carer groups and to train nurses and social workers.

When we talk about 'cutting', this kind of self harm can evoke strong reactions of shock, anger, disgust and reveal misunderstanding and judgemental attitudes. I try to help people to see that the majority of us engage in some behaviour that isn't good for us – the classic examples being smoking, drinking too much and eating too much or too little. The difference is that these types of self harm are more socially acceptable.

I was certainly shocked and disgusted at my own self harm at first. It's taken a very long time to understand and accept that I had to self harm, as I knew no other way to cope. I now have to live with the legacy of scars and a damaged arm which I still feel the need to hide. When I see my scars, I feel overwhelmed by all the pain they represent. However they are my battle scars and my writing this piece is evidence that the battle did not end in defeat.

I'm not sure if I'll ever lose the vulnerability to self harm, but as each day passes and as I face the many challenges of life; I know that I am stronger and know that I do now have, hope and a future.

By Angela Warren

Illustration by John Housley

When Pain came to stay

Marie Williams

I am old and grey, and wiser now,
But does the pain go away?
No it stays another day.
Why does it stay for another day?
When I want this pain to go away?

This pain has been my friend
He moved in with me many years ago
I don't remember asking him to stay
In fact I barely knew his name
But he took the best room in the house

I was only 5 when Pain knocked on the door
"Who are you", I said, no screamed!
A kick, then a punch, and my body flew
Through the air, Pain was not happy
To leave it there, He needed to leave his mark

Seemed like hours and hours
The hurt and the struggle
Knocking me, knocking me
Hurting me, the tears and the fears
Were born that day

And how that child pain grew
From strength to strength
And day to day, what could I do
To make pain pack his bags and leave
So that I could be so happy and free

I'll never know why Pain chose me
I guess that will always be a mystery
All I know is that it fed off me
And almost brought me to death's door
The day pain came to stay with me

At last Pain has decided to go
And will I miss Him? Oh gosh no!
But am I stronger for his stay; did I triumph after all?
Put it this way, the locks to that door have been changed
And Pain no longer holds a key

Illustration by Lorna Gillam

Alicia Gomez

scars

To paint me in perfection
would you include the scars?

Or would my skin be smooth
and even as caramel and twice as swee

Loving me would be loving them
and imperfections would be glorious
flames of beauty that shape
Me.

In paints, pastels or pencil
they would be there
perfectly.

Ray's Rambles

by Ray

So many issues fill my head all the time about this aspect of me, shame, disgust, guilt as well as practical things like how long can I keep lying to my son about the marks on my arms when we go swimming? When I go away on my own for a break from my life as a carer should I pack dressings and savlon? There are times when I hate myself, and times when I am able to relax.

Days, weeks, months and years have been lost trying to get my head round this, why do I feel the need to hurt myself? You cut yourself up for cutting yourself up. I have decided not to rationalise this any more, it's just what I sometimes do. I know it's not good but you can waste your life trying to rationalise the irrational. Learn to live with it and don't give yourself a hard time. Easier said than done though.

The feelings you get are frightening and upsetting. I can only describe it as an overwhelming feeling of despair, literally enveloped in pain and grief, and sometimes when you hurt yourself you feel an immediate release, this is only temporary. You go into a sort of zone, cleaning yourself up is some sort of ironic looking after yourself exercise. I am lucky that I have never had to seek immediate medical attention, that must be really scary. It possibly helps that I have previously trained as a nurse and can look after myself, but it also gives me an insight into some negative and hurtful attitudes that people who self harm encounter at Accident and Emergency Departments.

Sometimes you can feel it coming on, things seem to crush you, you feel a ball of something in your stomach and you just know that you will soon self harm. Should you fight it? Should you give in to it? I don't think that there is a right or wrong answer to these questions. I suppose that I'm learning to accept it. It's great when

I go for long periods of time without hurting myself, but I know that I will do it again. I think that this is my first step to self help rather than self harm.

I am embarrassed by my behaviour, I try not to be, but I have definitely found telling people helps. Obviously I am very, very selective about who I confide in. I told my GP, who was fantastic, understanding and supportive. I know that not all GP's have such insight and dedication, so I am not recommending people do this as a matter of course. I have talked to a few very close friends and their response has been awesome and most importantly non judgemental. For personal reasons I have not told any members of my family, apart from my wife, who I share an open honest relationship with.

I think like many difficulties that people face, self harm is not perceived correctly or kindly by society in general. I asked about books on self harm in a large bookshop recently and was directed to the teenagers section. Don't get me wrong, it's positive that teenagers get recognition, but it's not helpful to them or others that self harm is seen as only a young person's problem. I don't know why the perception of people who behave as I do is that we are all attention seeking, pain loving, hysterical young girls. Maybe it's easier to compartmentalise then ignore us.

I know that I'm going to struggle with this for a long time yet. But I also think that I'm going to be OK. As I have already said, stopping trying to make sense of it has helped enormously. It doesn't make sense, but it is a coping mechanism; not to damage yourself, but to survive. No it's probably not the best thing to do but it is not a choice. Anyone who says so is at best suffering more themselves from a complete lack of empathy.

My love, respect and best wishes go out to anyone who behaves, or is affected by anyone who behaves as I do. We are men, women, young, old and represent every social class, ethnic background and sexual orientation. Good luck with it and give yourself a break every now and again.

Illustration by Caroline Roe

Julia's Story

Julia Samuels

My daughter told me that she was self harming when she was 13 years old. Initially it followed the breakdown of a close friendship she had lost suddenly and without warning (Although retrospectively I think there were other, deeper rooted issues). The end of this friendship mortified her. She is very introvert as a personality which made it hard for her to contain and as well talk about her feelings. She voluntarily showed me her arms, which were covered in cuts. I tried to contain my horror, I think quite successfully, at the sight of my little girl covered in self inflicted cuts. But I was shaken with fear of what state of mind she must have been in, shocked at the sight of her injuries. Naive as it sounds, I thought 'why?', 'how could things have got so bad?', and 'how could she be feeling that sad?'

"My instinct was to protect her."

I knew she was feeling desperate, and there I was, with an unbelievable sense of shame and guilt (where did I go wrong?), and powerlessness. I just didn't know what to do. I never showed her how upset I felt. I was her rock; I couldn't show her my own vulnerability. I cried in private, I felt hopeless and helpless, very, very alone, and I had to carry on with my own life, as if everything was normal. It's not something people talk about. This is something that happens to other people, it's hidden, under the carpet and doesn't fit into everyday conversation.

My instinct was to protect her, I wanted to go back to when she was a baby, nurse her as if she was sick. We spent more time together, talking, going out, whatever she wanted to do really. I learnt a lot about self injury through reading and researching, and through observing and talking to my daughter I learned what it meant to her. She told me amongst other things, that it was her way of gaining some order and control, in a world that she experienced as unpredictable and painful. She didn't want help with it, she just wanted understanding, and that's what I tried to do. This is and always has been the hardest thing for me to accept and deal with. I wanted her to stop self harming, but she wasn't and still is not ready to. You have to be more than understanding sometimes.

I did get professional help for her - she and I regularly visit the Children and Mental Health Team. She also sees the GP, but the thought of medication terrifies her, as does the thought of change. So we are stuck, at least for the moment. It has been more than 3 years now since my daughter started self harming, and despite the professional and family input, I have had to accept that this is where she is, she just isn't ready to change, not yet.

As a person and parent I have changed though. I don't cry any more, although I sometimes do still get deep, uncomfortable feelings of desperation, grief and guilt. I feel closer in many ways to my daughter, more knowledgeable about her as a sensitive individual, still growing, learning and coping with the fragility of life and relationships. I really don't know if she will ever feel able or ready to change her way of coping- that is something I have to live with. But I will never stop caring for her, trying to help her find some form of motivation or support that she will feel able to accept. I'm still hopeful that the answers that are right for her are out there. I don't know whether society knows how to cope with this influx of young people who take their pain out on themselves. What I do know is that I will never give up on her.

Photograph by Caroline Roe

Working with young people who self-harm

Author: Marie Armstrong, Nurse Consultant, CAMHS - Self-harm team
Registered Child and Adolescent Mental Health Nurse & Systemic Family/Psychotherapist

I love working with young people. The privilege of hearing their stories and struggles, that are sometimes harrowing and very difficult to hear, never leaves me. When young people self-harm it can become an additional problem on top of the underlying problems that led them to self-harm in the first place. Working together with them, at their pace, towards their goals is very rewarding. In health care we are encouraged to use outcome measures, as there is a pressure to 'evidence' if what we are doing is working. Whilst this can be useful there is nothing as powerful as hearing directly from the young people when they are beginning to think, feel and behave differently.

"I would never have believed before coming to the group that I could even think about stopping cutting myself. Now I know I can". Lauren age 17

"I could have taken the easy route, my GP wanted to put me on anti-depressants, but I said no and look at me now"! (Smiling, happy, no self-harm). Lisa age 17

Believing in the young person and holding onto hope is essential. It is important to 'be with' the young person, understand the place they are in and how difficult things are for them whilst at the same time believing that things can change and they can take control of some things in their lives in order to make positive changes. This balance is hard to gauge so feedback from the young person is vital. In the context of a trusting therapeutic relationship, they will let you know if they feel they are being challenged and supported too much or too little.

Growing Pains

Alexander Worth

Slash. That's what we labelled her, the
girl in our class who seldom spoke but was
always there, tales of her troubles
carved into twig arms. She was kept
in the dark, but no one cared and
no one would listen. Tormented by the
teasing and closed ears, she ran. She ran until
twenty years later, the seasons reunited us and the
scars still remain. The bearer is
no longer fragile, but stands tall like an
oak tree, foundations rooted into love. No
sapling such as I could ever break through the
bark, her branches creaking of maturity as
I am hidden below them, forever
to remain a weed, waiting to be
pulled from the earth and finally into
sweet redemption.

Biography
Hey, my name's Alexander Worth from Wales, UK.
I'm 16, and I've grown up around a few self-harmers
who I've thankfully helped pass through bad times.

Photograph by Caroline Roe

Life by The Power of Two

Anne Garland

For Caroline

I have been asked to make a contribution to this book from the perspective of a professional. I am a mental health nurse who is also trained in cognitive-behavioural psychotherapy, which I have practised for the last twenty years. When I was asked to write about my professional views on self-harm for a while I was stuck. I then began to reflect on all the people with whom I have worked with in a professional capacity where self-harm has been part of their story. I work in a psychotherapy team and as a result I have a particular experience of working with self-harm, overwhelmingly in the context of childhood sexual abuse and adult trauma. Usually the person seeking help struggles with the very act of therapy because of the betrayal of trust inherent in abuse experiences and the need for trust in any therapeutic encounter. As a therapist something that always resonates when working with issues of self-harm is the self-blame and self-loathing that the person carries and how this colours their entire sense of self and their engagement in the therapy process. To survive we need hope and for many people with whom I work this is often fragile and frequently obscured or seemingly lost. I see my role as a therapist is to instil hope and when hope is obscured by pain and fear and agonising memories it is my job to hold that hope for both of us. With hope comes light and salvation.

In my deliberations on how to approach the task at hand I chose to write a poem. For me this medium captures a more intricate and complex meaning and allows an exploration of meaning at the level of felt sense. In the context of self-harm what lies beneath the act itself is the heart of the matter and this is often both complex and seemingly contradictory. What I have tried to convey in the poem is the temporary obscuring of hope and need for validation, acceptance, predictability and reliability on the part of the therapist in order to restore hope. Ultimately hope is a precious gift, which needs to be nurtured, alongside an understanding of the darkness that can prevail to obscure its light and the internal pain which at times overwhelms and for which help is necessary. It is the readers' judgment on as to how I succeeded in this endeavour.

This place, here now
pitch black, stone cold
numb to the bone with fear.
breathing death's vapour
alone, abandoned.

A gentle knocking
at your heart
a sure, defiant whisper
let me in; I'm here to help.
It can be done.

The demon rouses
bars the way, guarding the secrets
swallowed long ago.

She lifts the light and
lets the shadow fall where it needs.
We listen
with intent, to palpable fear.

Your face, illuminated, motionless,
save the flicker of a knowing eye.
He's here, you gasp, I feel his menace.
Help me, please don't go.

The fractured and
divided self splinters.
The terrorised woman is begging, pleading
the angry girl is shouting, fighting.
And underneath the broken child is weeping.

His venom takes hold
a visceral possession speaks his words:
My fault, I make him do this
I am bad
A bitch-slut, rotten, stinking
I am nothing, let me be
I deserve to die.

Be gentle with yourself she asks;
Take my hand, she coaxes.
Let's walk a while together,
She lifts the flame to light the path ahead.

What is the point?
There is no end
Each day tormented by
perpetrated atrocities relived.
Self-loathing sets, flesh and bone against itself.
Starve the body, debased and defiled.
Cut out the evil and purge the poisonous bile.
Slake the fear with liquid and with pill.
Holding up the light to look ahead
there is another way she says.

A path as yet untrodden
it is long and we would have to
help each other.
Some terrain, the quicksand and the wastelands
I know from other journeys,
but the twists and turns and switchbacks
these we need to navigate together.

What do you say?
Why do you bother?
Are you mad at me?
Do you hate me?
I am too much in every way.
You will eventually get sick of me and leave.
You have to, your care and concern is pain
beyond compare.

I know she says, handing you the light,
This is the price you pay for their betrayal.
Each fragile brokered trust too easily shattered.
Alone and frightened.
All hope lost.
And in this silenced and solitarily space
death raises her siren song and shame
casts your gaze away from this compass light.
Look at the light it is yours now too, use it as you will.
Touch it, taste it, smell it.
How does it feel? Listen, what does it sing?
And let this be your solace and your guide.

Hope

A reply

There was blackness
always had been, dark
and the landscape of my life, bleak.
I hid behind all I found.
I ran, wherever running took me
and then you came
(though I don't remember you finding me)

You were there.
You listened without forsaking
I began to give without you taking;
the storms stilled.
Though the wind shrieked with memories
and threatened to bring in the world,
you believed and kept believing.
I began to see through your eyes;
That in darkness there are stars.
With your help I stood, with help,
and took my first tentative steps
into the uncertain...

Whilst my tears stained our path
and paddled the ground
you waited for the storm to quieten.
Flowers grew at my feet
Where the tears had fallen.
The land was now rich
and you held my hand, patiently
until I could show my face and turn to the spring

Away from the winter that I had been
I wept once more, but this time
For Hope.

By Caroline Roe

Let me care.

Elizabeth Prasse

Photograph by Dana Boulton

what do you say...
        when someone says they're dying?
                ... I feel that way too sometimes

what do you do...
        when they pull away from everyone?
                ... I want to hide away myself

do we reach out or give them space?
do we follow or do we fade?

spending countless hours contemplating...

undone

I want to care...
        when they want me, when they don't
            ... let me care

I feel like I'm back in that dark, lonely hole
My increased harm, destroying my soul,
Every day, every hour, the urge gets too much,
I'm fighting myself, my wounds I cant' touch.

What am I doing to myself, I ask?
The problem is now self-harm is my task,
Constant bad thoughts of my family I fear,
the need to self-harm to keep them near.

The pains from the past come into light,
now it's a case of fight or take flight.
Yes, I've been here fair few times before,
now I feel tired, exhausted and sore.

My mother, my siblings, I love them so much;
sadly, with Dad, love doesn't count such.
God, if you're listening, please help me out,
Inside I'm screaming, unable to shout.

PLEASE UNDERSTAND ME AND NOT THE SELF-HARM;
it's too complicated for me to stay calm.
My one wish in life- find the real me,
when that day comes, I'll finally be free.

Dear God

By Julie

unscathed

Alicia Gomez

I always frown
when I look in the mirror at my back.
I half expect to see a sea of scar--
dark lattice of shiny keloid.

But they can't see anything there from that night,
just the tan of my ethnic.
They don't know what I'm looking for
call me lucky to have such beautiful skin.
It pulls a long sigh from me. How do I say:

I would gladly bare,
under the burning sun,
the scar of once melted flesh

If only so people would remember
I was there too.

Cold and Alone

D J Crimson

Nowhere to go; the house is too small to disappear from; my room is no longer mine. They try to talk to me but all I want is to be alone, I want so badly to be alone. I rush to the bathroom, lock the door, keep the light turned out (the lights hurt my eyes too much). With my back to the door I slide down until I'm a little ball on the tiled floor. The cold seeps into me and I feel like I'm turning to stone. The pain builds up inside and the tears start falling. I can't stop them; I bite my hands to stop the moans that escape my throat. I rock back and forth, as my mind attacks me again and again. The pain builds up and I tell myself how worthless I am; how pathetic, how alone, how no one likes me, how I'll always be alone...

I try not to make a sound. It's my mind versus me, and I could never stand up to myself. I hear them laughing and it feels like they are mocking me. I slam my head backward with all my strength into the wall, it hits with a crack. The pain shoots from the back of my head to my temples, like an electric crown. My head throbs, but I do it again.

My tears stop and I manage to stop moaning. For a second I am calm.

I wish he could be here with me, he'd know how to make it alright. He's not allowed near me anymore, he's kept away from me and I can't even call him.

I want to end.

Cracking my head against the wall…

Unwanted Soul - Amil Solanke

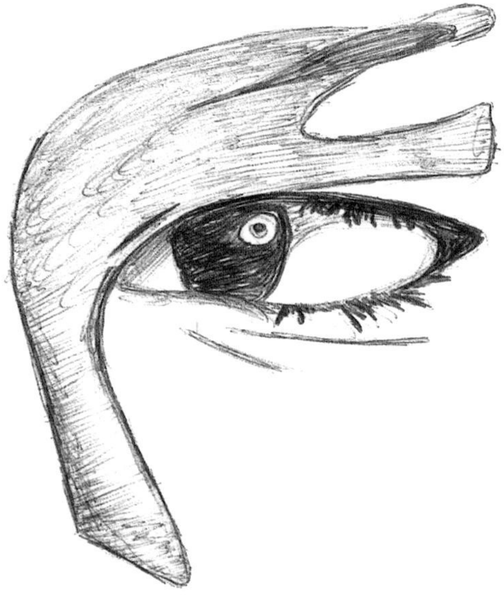

Illustration by Lorna Gillam

Shame

By Claire Hayes

I can see it in their eyes-- the disappointment. In my mother's eyes I also see anger. But in my father's eyes, I can see something worse; fear.

Why can't they see that this isn't because of them? This was never about them. I love them so much, I never wanted to put them through this, but I'm terrified of what I might do if I'm left alone.

My arms are stinging now, as I feel the shame starting to burn on my face. What have I done? I could never tell them of the abuse, the agony of the secrets I've had to keep for so long. The pain on the inside was killing me far more than any pain I could ever cause myself.

She asks me why. I cannot answer. The secrets holding my tongue as her eyes drop to the floor.

He tells me it's their fault. He says they have failed as my parents. I can't look at him now.

I've hurt them more than I could ever hurt myself. A moment of release would never have been worth a lifetime of thinking that I had made my mom and dad hate me.

Self Harm: My Story

Rachel Anderson

I'm 32 and I started harming myself in my teens, possibly earlier if I'm honest. The main trigger being the sudden and devastating loss of someone close to me. When I cut for the first time I felt a range of emotions but interestingly, felt that it had been the right thing to do – it worked; it made me feel better instantly and relieved the emotional burden that I was struggling to cope with by turning it into something physical. The physical pain could be contained – unlike the emotional pain. I cut myself and it helped; it helped me communicate my distress and cope with the unbearable.

Several years ago I remember being in hospital following an overdose. It wasn't a suicide attempt just a way of trying to hide away from things for a while. In reference to me I heard 'well she's obviously been sexually abused'. A common perception I'm sure but although there is a strong correlation between self harm and sexual abuse I personally was never sexually abused. I do however, self harm. The point I am making here is that it is unhelpful to make assumptions about why people self harm. For me self harm was (and still is) about staying alive and dealing with emotions that are too intense or painful or confusing to vocalise.

Self harm can provoke intense reactions of anger but hopefully it can also provoke feelings of compassion and understanding in others; others who have been there themselves or who would like to help. Self harm is a journey and for everyone out there a different journey. It is not necessary to label people like me as 'self harmers' because that undermines the rest of who we are and what we stand for. We are just like others who choose not to cut themselves. We use a coping method that works for us, if not being a little different from the norm. Different, however, doesn't have to mean wrong. Whilst it works to help some people cope with emotional distress and tension it shouldn't be taken away from them. When a person is ready to leave self harm behind, more often than not they do.

Incidentally, as my journey continues I hold down a full time job, pay a mortgage and have a loving partner. There are many others like me. Years ago I couldn't see a point in living but that has changed - it is possible to come out the other side and to cope with life 'just like anybody else.'

Biography: Rachel has been a member of the editorial group for this project.

Photograph by John Housley

JUST ONE STEP (MORE)

BY ELAINE LO

When you're in the middle of it, you don't know what's happening. In fact, you're oblivious. Only when you've escaped, you see what it truly is; the lies, the deceptions, the charades toying with your mind, making your emotions screw in a tangle, a black void.

We deal with this in many ways. One way, for me, was self-harm.

I started self-harming when everything collapsed around me, from an abusive relationship with a friend to my mother. I remember all the hate and all the pain; there was so much pain. I kept asking the question 'Why?' Sometimes I directed it at myself, sometimes at God. They were three letters that meant so, so much.

At that time, I hadn't discovered music, my life-line. Nor did I discover much of anything else. I didn't know what options laid out before me and I was also narrow-minded.

Nobody was there for me physically, so I had no one to rely on. I guess I made the decision to never trust anyone completely and to remain alone on that day as well. I learnt to cope with the loneliness, but only the physical loneliness. The mental and emotional loneliness could never be scraped away so easily.

Self-harm was one way to express that mental and emotional loneliness. Sometimes I had to see it physically to still believe I was still alive, that I was still living a life. The only thing I could rely on were the people online. They slowly affected my life and I began to change. It took a while, I admit it. It took a heck of a long time and a heck of a load of patience, but they were there. They didn't stand next to me. They didn't give me hugs and no, I couldn't hear them. They stood by me mentally and emotionally though. They pushed and continued to have faith in me.

I guess what I'm trying to say is you're never alone. Even if you are alone physically, you're not mentally or emotionally. There will always be people who care and there will always be people who will have faith.

It is safer to isolate yourself when you are in intense pain, whether physically, mentally or emotionally. But if you just try and seek help, perhaps open yourself a tiny bit, you will see. You will see all these people waiting to guide you to a life that doesn't have to include self-harm. For me, I met people who showed me how great I was. Even though I am still suffering from feelings of inferiority and insignificance, I know now that there are people who care and who are willing to help me every step of the way.

Keep the Faith.

21st century canvas

Louise Nightingale

My body is a canvas
A piece of modern art
The scars, they tell a story
Reveal pain inside my heart

The blood red as a ruby
My skin as white as snow
The contrast is so striking
With a frightening angry glow

People stop to look at it
But no one seems to care
To look beyond the canvas
At the person standing there

A girl who longs to be noticed
Who is shadowed by her pain
The girl known as the canvas
The artwork with no name

But if they were to stop a while
Much more than art they'd see
A girl with many feelings
Hopes, wishes and dreams

Illustration - Lace by Julie Fordham

we
calm
no word
together
in no place
filling in a space
that time would jump
no word about the world
that talks about the weather
in the cafe by the rubbish dump
a serentan refuge where we're curled
breathes softly in the ripples of the sea
I'm sure you'd start to think this is absurd
and I am convinced we never did do any harm
but then you'd say this doesn't have to come from me

stasis

Stasis

Rodney Yates

I won't write this for you

Julie Bouchonville

I won't ask you why; I don't care.
I won't say it's wrong; you don't care.
I won't judge you; I dislike wasting my time.
I won't say I know what it feels like; I could be lying.
I won't ask you to tell your story; it's not my business.
I won't ask you how; it's obvious.
I won't talk with kindness; I'm not a kind person.
I won't call you stupid, egoist, or fool; you're not.
I won't beg for you not to do it again; why would you listen?
I won't say I understand; it wouldn't make you feel better.
I won't remind you of your friends or your family; they're constantly on your mind.
I won't talk about the little birds, the flowers, or the sun. You wouldn't even hear.
I won't say you're strong or that you can overcome.

You wouldn't believe me.

But what will I say?
I'll hold you.
I won't let you down.
I'm here.
It's all over.
You're not alone. Not anymore.

And you won't hear, won't listen or won't believe- but you'll know it. And that's already a good beginning.

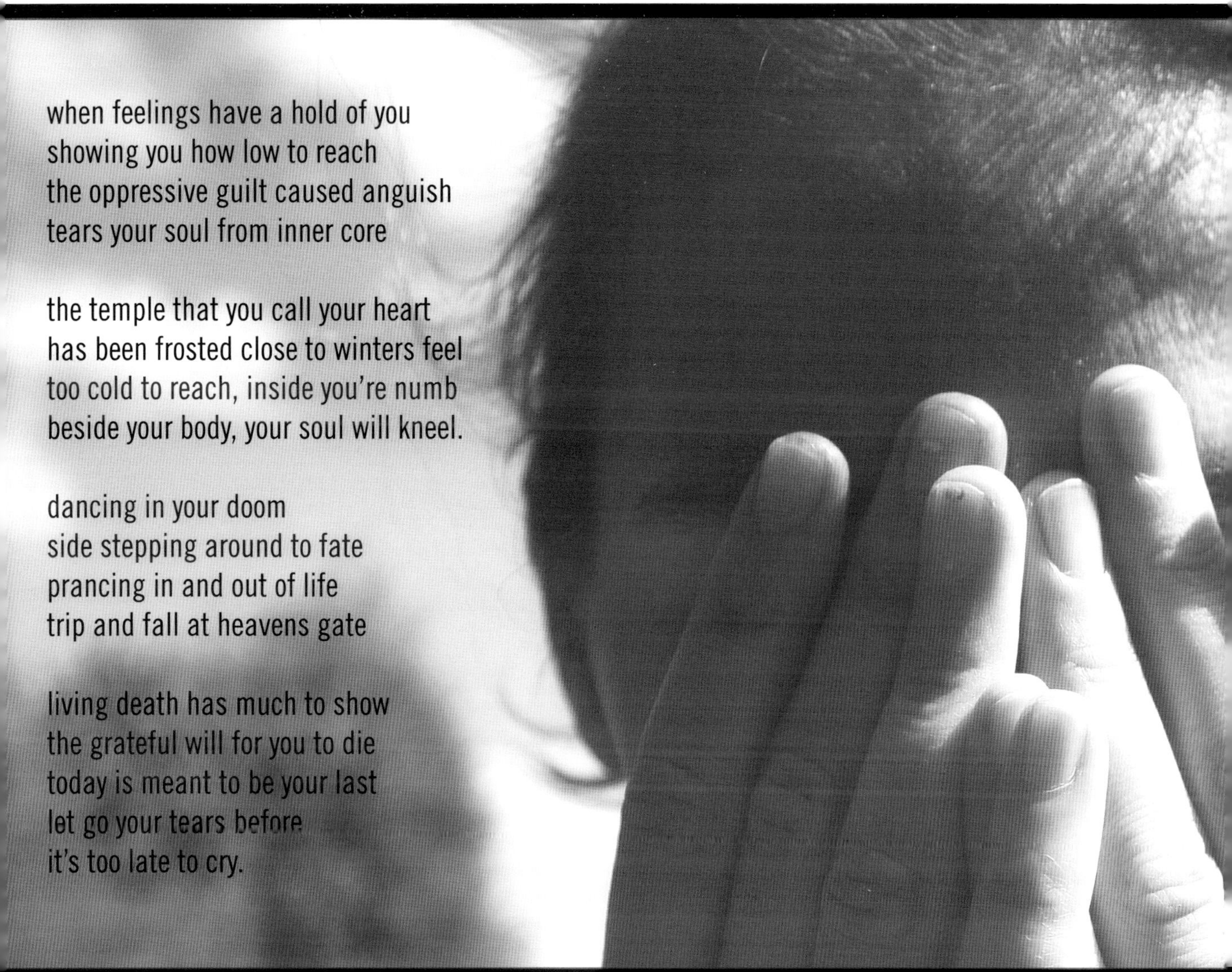

when feelings have a hold of you
showing you how low to reach
the oppressive guilt caused anguish
tears your soul from inner core

the temple that you call your heart
has been frosted close to winters feel
too cold to reach, inside you're numb
beside your body, your soul will kneel.

dancing in your doom
side stepping around to fate
prancing in and out of life
trip and fall at heavens gate

living death has much to show
the grateful will for you to die
today is meant to be your last
let go your tears before
it's too late to cry.

Do not miss your chance to cry

Silver Dae

Photograph by Amy Harris

Illustration by John Housley

Healed

Lee McCabe

My past is a jagged line,
littered with blood.
Words of the heart and mind
Tears of sorrow, regret and relief
slowly turned the deep angry scar
from bitter red to deep hues of pink.
Time, passing constantly evolves it
to the white of cleaned bone
'till you realize that the ache
once so deep has passed. Even healed,
though never forgotten.
A white line remaining, a
reminder of courage needed
to live life.

Addiction by Michael Crawford

Untitled

Hayley Smith

Surrounded by masses who could not comment
They whispered to each other without speaking a word
I have been here many times, trapped in this torment
Shouting my voice, never being heard

I open my soul to search for calm
When I found her, she was hiding inside
She didn't mean for me to come to harm
Fear had been chasing, she was trying to hide

I asked her to stay, to give me comfort
To help me with feelings I can not defeat
I was relieved to feel the outpouring of hurt
I slept and my heart became a regular beat

Hands and Leaf by Amna Ahmed

Calm slipped away, left me at the dead of night
She always leaves and I beg her to stay
I awoke with panic back, blocking out the light
I closed my eyes and asked for a better day

Soon I will go searching for calm again
She hides further away now, fear is too strong
I search deep inside for a respite from pain
But when I find her again, she won't stay for long

Dear Darkness
By Shawn Hansen

Photograph by Amy Harris

Fortitude

by MSJames

The willow bends away
bends away from the wind,
the wind bends everything
everything to its will,
its will cannot be broken
be broken by the willow,
the willow bends away.

Kayla Desroches

I Grew Resilience

I decided to name my tree 'Amelia'. After searching through 'How to Name That Baby' the night before, I planned out exactly how to gain the proper amount of privacy for the next day. It all worked out surprisingly well.

I pretended to be sleeping so that my grandmother could not trap me into going furniture shopping. I remembered how, when I first moved in, she insisted on buying me a carpet in the town thrift shop that resembled the fur sprouting from an ape's feet, red and patchy. I felt proud of myself. For both gaining an opportunity to plant Amelia and for avoiding a trip back to that place.

I knew where to get my supplies. I picked up the half bag of nutrient enriched soil and my collection of acorns from the garage, both of which I had stashed behind the three large boxes of grandma's special gum. I had no idea the gum would be so useful when grandma first bought it.

The TV advertised it as the 'NUMBER ONE WAY TO QUIT SMOKING NOW! GET RESULTS IN TWO MONTHS OR YOUR MONEY BACK!' The producers hired an actor with bleached teeth and a severe overbite, as if they wanted to make sure his teeth would always hang out to show their cleanliness. He probably popped ten mints into his mouth before filming, just to make sure we could smell the freshness through the screen. The clogged, liquid drain cough of smokers would have gone well with his watery eyes, and I bet his name was something like Pip or Norman. I wouldn't trust the origins of those names.

I liked to think that Amelia's namesake promised success through hard work and perseverance, but the name itself meant striving and industrious. I'd tried to plant three trees before this one, once at my parent's house and twice at my aunt's. All three failed before they reached the air. My aunt had uprooted my last attempt. She didn't see the point in growing a tree for a child who wasn't living with her. In any case, grandma seemed to provide much more promising grounds for Amelia.

She owned a clean cut garden which would be perfect for planting the tree after it grew to a reasonable height inside the house. I had plans to defend against the school security guard who lived next to grandma. He threw empty beer bottles all over the place, and once or twice I found crunched cans under the bushes near our back door. I only spotted the ones he overlooked in his sessions of his early morning clean-ups, during which he crept around his neighbors' yards and picked up all the cans he had emptied the night before.

You wouldn't think a tree could grow up next to such a bad influence, but I planned to build a fence around the little baby. Perhaps I would buy a metal gate, which would serve strong enough to hold back the bumbling body of a falling drunk. I didn't want the little tree smashed under our neighbor's large behind.

When I had all the materials, I set them up on grandma's shell-pink counter and pulled the printed directions from my jean pocket. I spread the paper out on the table and pressed the creases with my thumbs.

1. Get a Styrofoam cup.

I pulled a cup from the stack next to the toaster and placed it beside the watering can.

2. Get a pencil

I laid a pencil next to the watering can and cup, all neat in a line.

3. With the tip of your sharpened pencil, poke three to four holes around the bottom of the cup.

I jabbed four holes near the base of the cup and replaced the number two pencil in the line of materials.

4. Fill the cup with soil, but leave an inch of room from the top for watering space.

I removed the clamp which held the bag of dirt closed and dipped the cup into the mass of soft, dark earth. The cup emerged with what looked like an ant colony on top, so I levelled it like one would a teaspoon of sugar before dumping it in a batter. I kept on removing the soil until I had approximately the right amount of space between the dirt and the top of the cup.

5. Plant the acorn near the top of the soil.

I unsealed the zip locked bag of acorns and placed them in an army-like formation in front of me, arranging them so that the three large ones sat in back, and the three small ones sat in front. I surveyed the bunch and, after some worry (I was certain that choosing the wrong one would ruin its chances at life), I picked the small one at the far left of the front row. It barely covered the pad of my thumb, but it seemed strong, and it shone like a waxed car.

I dipped my pinky into the soil to make way for the acorn and slipped it into its nest like a little egg. I left it close enough to the top so that the stem still poked out.

6. Fill the cup with water to the top.

I filled the cup under the faucet and watched as the water disappeared into the soil as if sucked down by some creature. I filled it again, and the water dribbled out of the holes like a fountain. The result seemed apocalyptic, as if any diversion from the directions foreshadowed doom, but I would not be disheartened.

I found a plate into which the water could flood and clambered upstairs to place the acorn in my room. I chose a spot under the window facing south, where Amelia would always get sun and which could be easily viewed from my bed.

Sometime during the process of planting Amelia, I had regained that enthusiasm with which I planted the last three trees. I was sure that this time she would have enough sun and enough care. I knew that Amelia would be resilient, just as her namesake promised.

Dear Friend

Amna Ahmed

My name is Amna Ahmed and I am seventeen years old. I have been quietly struggling since the seventh grade and continue to do so.

Dear Friend,

I know that you are worried about me and wish that you could understand or be able to help me but at this point I want to stop from all the struggles and just let you know how much I love you. You're the best friend I could have asked for and even though there are days where I cannot get out of bed or times when you and I both know that we are pretending to be happy, pretending that we didn't hear my screams and sobs last night. And even though it's a warm summer day and I am wearing long sleeves and a jacket, even though I wince in pain every time the cloth runs over the mistakes we both know are hiding under my sleeve, neither of us acknowledge what I've done.

At this point it seems to be easier than trying to discuss it. There are so many triggers to avoid that discussing has become one of them. I wish I could be your strong girl as you have asked me to be. And I want to be strong for you. But when I see eyes shift to my arm and look at me like a freak, when my own cousin condemns me as a nonbeliever, when someone doesn't understand how I could have possibly drawn that into my skin, I cannot stand on my two feet with my chin raised. I am afraid. The confidence, the strength, the bravery the public sees is my mask. I pretend in front of everyone because I am afraid to be weak.

Life is so terrible. So many people are hurt, in accidents and wars, in poverty and oppression. Why should the world stop because I am too weak to let go of the little things that stuck to me and wear me down? I am nothing special, just one more face to add to the crowd. Let me struggle in silence and save someone who cannot stop what is happening to them, whose struggle is not abstract but a force that can be stopped. There are others who need help more than I do. Who would be grateful, thankful, for the littlest of aid. But you choose to help me? You choose to hold me in your arms, comfort me when my thoughts haunt me and the nightmares do not leave even when I am awake. You try to quiet the pain. Sometimes it stops the urge. But when I am alone with that cursed piece of silver I need to release the emotional pain from myself so I can be in peace.

The addiction, the blessed feeling of release that I so crave and desire when I am at my wit's end undermines the love you fill into my empty being. I am not trying to hurt you; I swear I am truly sorry. I promise you that I do not hate you and that it is not your fault. I truly do try to get better for you but I ask of you to please understand that this is my way of dealing with the struggles in my life. I try to get better for you and although there are times when I seem not to be myself and scream at you, hurt you in so many ways, and confuse you as you try to comfort me and suffice my needs, I want you to try and remember the small happy moments we have shared with one another.

I am not trying to take my life from you. I never asked for you to become my friend, I am blessed to have you. This is tough for me. I am supposed to be stronger than this and able to handle my problems reasonably. Yet I am weak; so pitifully weak. I am only a child trapped by my own complex twisted justifications. I know that I deserve to be hurt and there are moments where it does not matter what I am told; my stubborn self will refuse reason and will only accept what I have condemned myself to. But I am fighting, fighting myself and fighting my desires. Some days are easy. Those days, I am free. Other days are harder and resisting the urge is all I can think of, part of my mind telling me to do it, a chunk reminding how much it hurts you, a part telling me that I know I deserve it, another saying no, and a small portion knowing that resisting is inevitable.

Your love helps me. The little things you do. Knowing that you care so much for me makes it easier to stop. It helps me fight. I love you so much for helping me become stronger. I know that I am not alone, regardless of how I feel. I know that you are there for me. So forgive me of the words I may have thrown at you during the many of my fits. Forgive me for hurting you, for the stripes and twists that mark me, for the times I tore myself from your side. I know that one day I will be strong enough and this will stop, the fight will be over, that I will have won, and we can smile together. Until then, I give you these words of hope.

With Love.

Daisy Chains

She picked a daisy carelessly;
touching the white petals
with her finger.
She gave it a gentle brush,
before sighing profound
with fond reflection.

"Remember when we made daisy chains?"
She asks with childlike wonder,
"When we were fairy queens
or bridal maidens,
walking down the grass aisle,
with buttercup bouquets
and dandelion rings to exchange?"

"I remember" I reply,
as I lie back in my own daydreams.
In this same field we used to play,
handstands and cartwheels.
We'd dance amongst the pollen
of dandelion clocks;
just like fairy queens.
Wearing only the natural props of
hand picked flowers to play out,
using our imagination.

"We had fun, didn't we?"
She sighs again.
"Where did it all go?
Our fantasy no longer exists;
we're too old for fairy queens"
She lies down next to me
upon the grass; despondent
by her own words.

"My friend," I reply, sitting back up.
I pick a daisy myself and grasp it
in my hand with defiance.
"We've grown into those fairy queens,
one day we'll be those brides!
Now this place is our haven;
our spot.
Do we not always come here to talk
when we are feeling low?
Or when we want to make decisions?
Or if you, like I, often come alone
to think and make daisy chains still
on my own?"

A smile upon her face as the child returns.
Her eyes watching the dandelion pollen
drift away in the gentle breeze.
"Of course I still make
daisy chains."

Rebecca Turney

Biography:
Rebecca has been a member
of the editorial group for this project.

My scars show I survived

Priscilla Turvey

You may see my scars and cringe, but you need to think that with those marks come some great and terrible tales.

My scars are more than just skin deep marks, they mean I survived.

My scars show that I survived all the years of being in pain, suffering, lessons learnt and moments of triumph.

I may have been forced to submit to others against my will, but these scars mark my path as things I have and continue to overcome.

I survived more than most people will ever experience.

I take my scars as they are and carry the stories they tell close to my heart, because I know without them I would not be who I now am. I would not have a tale written on me to tell and share my knowledge with the world.

I wear the mark of a survivor because I did what I had to in order to overcome and grow as a person.

Snow White by Tessa Bamkin

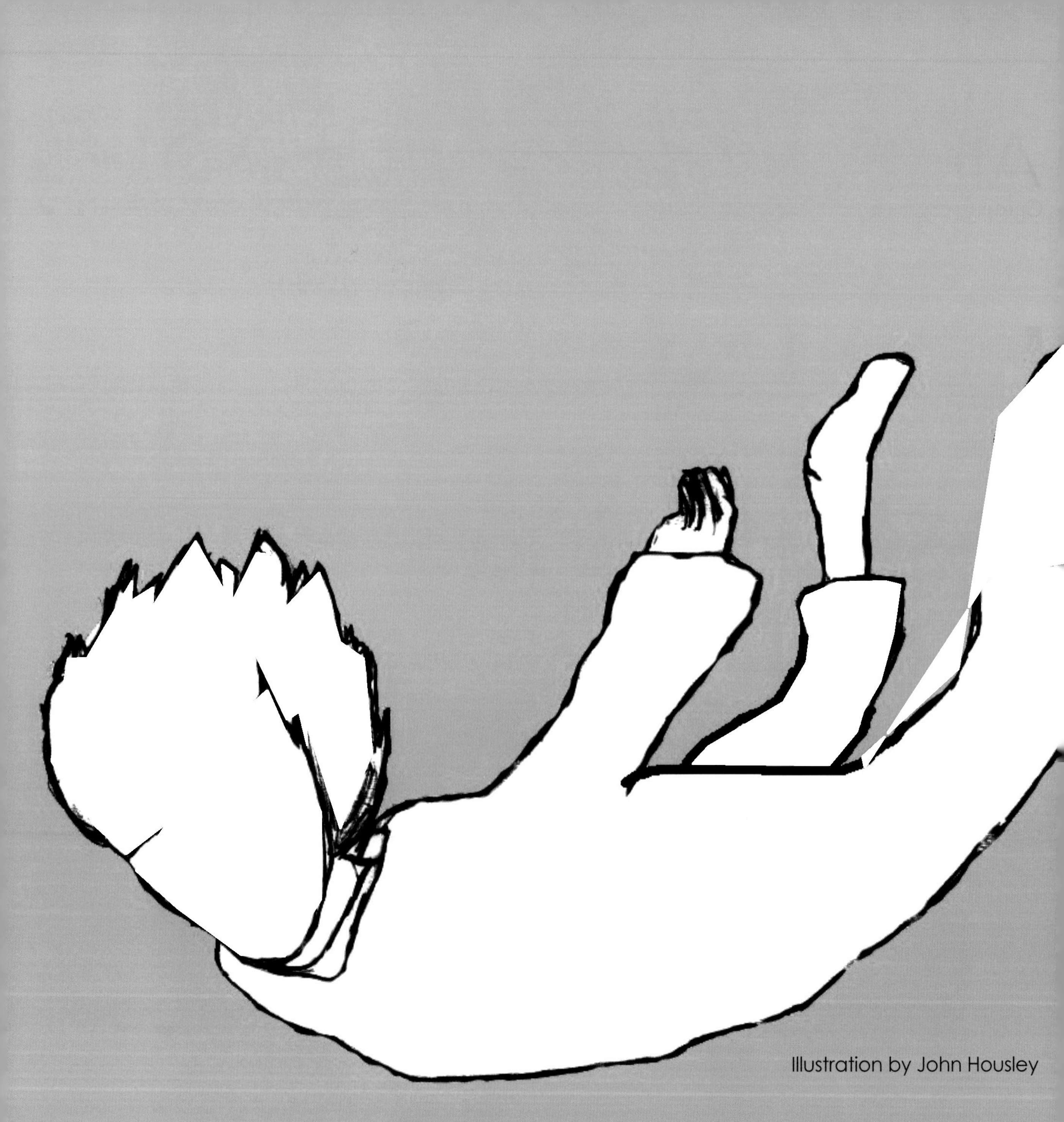

Illustration by John Housley

Alice in Wonderland

Caroline Smailes

Back then that Princess Diana and me was ill. It made it easier for me grandma and me granddad to understand. Princess Diana was bulimic and the grandbairn was too. It kind of made it ok, normal and almost good. I mean they didn't go round boasting, nothing like that, but if anyone was to ask what was wrong with the grandbairn and why I was in and out of hospital, well they'd say I was ill with what that Princess Diana had.

Back then I was sixteen and Alice, the girl who lived next door to me grandma and granddad, she was 'bout a year older than me. She was me friend for when I had to stay at me grandma and me granddad's house. We'd sit on her front wall and talk 'bout stuff. That's how she got to telling me 'bout how she hit her own arm with a hammer till it got all swollen and red and she had to go to hospital. She told me that her arm hurting made all the rubbish stuff in her life better. She said that she liked the pain, cos it made her feel normal 'stead of how sad she felt all the other time. I told her how I understood, cos I did. She told me 'bout her mam not bothering with her, but that when her arm was in a plaster cast her mam'd be all smiley and her mam'd talk to her and she'd not feel invisible no more. Then Alice told me 'bout how the pain cleared out the inside of her head, like the crying for her arm hurting made all the other pain inside of her better.

Back then Alice let me touch her hammer. We was sitting on her front wall and I had on me purple slippers, the ones with the fluffy lining. I touched Alice's hammer and it felt cold. I asked her how she did it, like how she was brave enough to hurt herself. She said she just kept on tap tap tapping till she could tap no more. Then she like tapped the hammer on her front wall to show me. She did like little taps first, then a big one that made a chip in the brick. That chips still there, like even now, like even after years.

Back then Alice told me that having real pain, a hurt that other folk could see, well she said it stopped people thinking she was a weird lass. I told her that I could never hurt meself like that. She told me that inside of her was like loads of secrets that made her want to scream and bang her head off the floor. She told me that the bloke from number fourteen had done like really sick things to her and her mam hadn't believed her when she'd tried to tell her 'bout it. I started crying and Alice laughed at me for being soft. She told me that sometimes she felt like she was going to explode and that the hammer made her feel better, like calmer. I told her 'bout me eating being rubbish and how I felt safe in hospital. I told her that I understood and 'bout how I was ill like that Princess Diana.

Back then, something like a year later, I was told that Alice was ill. It was almost in a whisper even though there was only me and me mam in the room. I think Alice had been ill for a few months and her mam had told me grandma cos she was sick with worry and knew that I'd been ill for a bit. I remember crying when I heard. It made me not want to talk to Alice no more. I'd sit at me grandma and granddad's window and I'd watch her through the net curtains and through the gap in me grandma's hedge.

Back then Alice went on a being ill longer than me. I mean that's what me mam and me grandma and me granddad thought. Alice didn't seem to be able to manage it, not like me. I mean I controlled it, pretended I was better when I wasn't and said what me mam and me grandma and me granddad wanted to hear. I didn't want them hassling me 'bout me illness. They was proud of me for getting better, like that Princess Diana did. Alice couldn't do that, she couldn't get better. She seemed to be anorexic for a bit and then bulimic for ages. She was in and out of the local psychiatric ward and she kept having plaster casts on her arm. She was all skin and bones. I never was. I think I envied her control and the way that the fat fell off. She was better than me at being ill.

Then, back then, it came out that Alice was having an affair with the husband of the daughter of the woman who lived opposite them. It got complicated. Alice was gossiped 'bout some more. I mean everyone on the estate found out 'bout Bulimic Alice, her hammer and how she was shagging a married bloke. People was always watching her and saying mean stuff about what type of lass she was. And I reckon that everyone knowing 'bout Alice made her be ill longer. I mean she was more on show but no one was asking her why she did all that stuff to herself. I mean, it's pretty obvious that all she wanted was for someone to help her. I mean I'm guessing, I don't know for sure and I can't ask her now.

Illustration by John Housley

Dear Taylor

Rebecca Renner

Biography:
I am a foreign language education student from the United States. This piece was made from a letter I wrote to someone very close to me. These words helped her find the strength within herself, and I hope they can do the same for others.

Dear Taylor,

You made me think about
what it really means to be beautiful.

I know I yelled at you
the first time you cut
in front of me. And we
put all the tacks
and scissors and paperclips
where you couldn't find them.

I didn't cry that night.
I know you did, but I didn't.
I didn't let myself.

But I did when I found the tacks
under your mattress
and the scratches on your knees.
I'm sorry I didn't tell anyone.

The next night, in the cabin
without any air-conditioning,
you told me how ugly you were.

That's something you
can only let me decide for myself.

You told me how much less
you mattered than everyone else.

"Why would I be listening to you
if you don't matter?"

It's not because it's my job.

It's because I see the woman
you will be someday, all the better for this.
You will fall in love despite your scars. And
someday you'll tell someone

just like you

that they are beautiful.

They're beautiful
because they help at the stables
and teach children how to use a camera.
They're beautiful
because they'd give up their seat
for another or hold a door open
or stand up for their friends.

Just like you,
they're beautiful, Taylor.
And you will see that beauty
every time they smile.

Please write back soon.

Strength

Sarah Clough

Illustration by Caroline Roe

What is strength?
Is it where you can stand up for yourself?
How do you truly know what it is?
Has anyone had strength?

Is strength where you can cope?
Is strength where you survive?
Is strength where you live?
Or is it where you give in?

So what is strength?
Maybe it is all of it
Maybe it is just one
who knows?

I think we are all strong
We all have strength here
Look at us,
We have all been through lots

We are still here
We are still going
Still living
That's strength

It takes a lot to go through what we have
We are all strong
We are survivors
We have survived

That's strength

Sometimes your life gets turned upside down; there is nothing you can do.
Sometimes if you try really hard, nobody sees the real you.
Sometimes you think your okay, when really you're falling apart.
Sometimes someone you thought you knew ends up breaking your heart.

Sometimes you forget what life is all about
You stay still sitting under clouds of doubt.
Fear grips your heart, hurt consumes your soul.
You build up walls to keep people out,
You live your life regretting because,
You can't get a grip on what you feel,
Darkness closes in on you, like an air tight seal

That is when you know *'sometimes'* has become a constant state
You punish yourself and end up hurting others
Because all you feel is hate.
You wish someone understood what you fight for every day
The memories within you don't go away

You want to reach out and trust but you're scared of the hurt
Making the people that you care for fall apart and walk away
They confront you because you don't know what to say
You retreat to your private prison and keep the hurt locked away.
Fighting to breathe, wanting just one happy day.

You are like me
You want to be happy and care free
You want to help others, to reach out
I ask you to see the child trapped deep inside,
That hides from pain.
You need to set them free allow your healing path to reveal

Those that were meant to protect you, you learnt not to trust
You're nearly an adult, but in yourself you're so lost.

Sometimes

Leah Liffen

Everything you were got taken away
Everything you want to be, something's always in the way
It's like a huge hole that gets bigger each day.
You think that if you ever speak you will fall apart
Dragging those down that you care for in your heart.

BUT

You will find someone that is willing to share
All the highs and laughter, to darkness and despair.
You may fight them trying to make them back away.
But it doesn't matter because they are stood there to fight with you;

If you dare to dream, let them care them you will see.

If you stand and fight
Give yourself a chance
Then you can truly open your heart.
To let healing begin.

The road is never easy
There are hard choices to be made
You'll come up against so much
You'll hurt, but you'll laugh too
It won't happen over night it is a long fight

With the right person by your side you can feel like you can fly
When you can look back and have no hurt, guilt or regret
You know with the people that you care for by your side,
You have truly healed from your past.

The Daisy

Alison Philbey

Sitting quietly in my deckchair
In the scorching summer sun,
I watched a little daisy
Tug gently – try to run
From something.
It seemed to be afraid;
Of what? I was not sure
But I could not sit and watch it
In its agony of war.

The trees' breeze held her back
But the sun it drew her on.
That daisy looked so ragged,
Pathetic and forlorn
That I had to stoop
To pick it up
And saw it in my hand:
Much happier now
From torment freed
With nothing now to dread,
I saw that it was more alive
Although, in fact, 'twas dead.

Illustration by Lorna Gillam

Still Life

S E Rene

Everyday you pose
stripped,
clothed,
identifying, mystifying.
You submit to the exposure,
resenting the attempts to iconify your soul--
now just a static blur, stamped into nature;
abused blues dyed in your melancholy.
Try to add colour to your desaturated self,
It's just a matter of time before you fade into someone else.
Just a matter of life-forming into a lost cause.

Step out the lines they've begun drawing,
and away from a mesmerizing paralysis--

Becoming your own canvas,
Embracing the pain;

still-life is worth it.

Squint

This morning I lean over the sink,
eyes half closed, dreams
undissolved
waiting for that familiar reflection--
behind me, the shampoo on the wall
squints into recognition;
together we greet the mirror
half empty.
I wonder how long I will have
to lather, rinse
repeat
until I'm in a better condition
to face myself today.
A hopeless smile peeks over
a corner of my raw lip, disturbed
as a peppermint sting
of froth flows down my throat.

Little girl

by Lucky

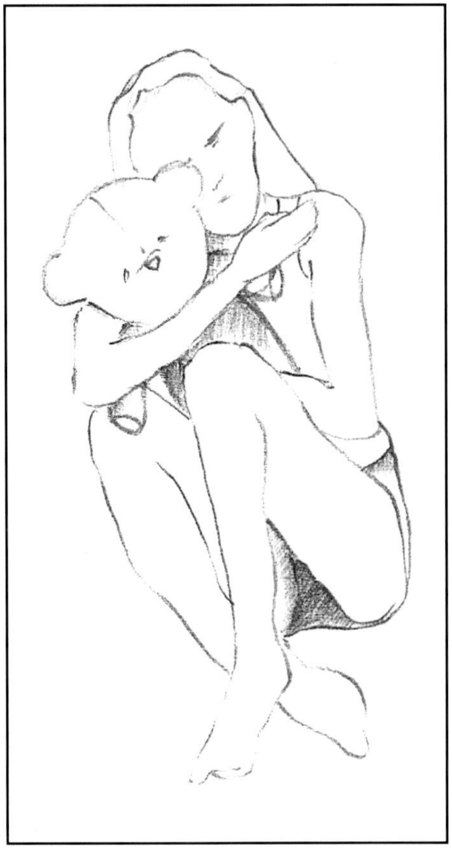

I see a little girl,
With a woman's eye,
She looks so frightened,
she's about to cry.
I would like to ask,
What it is that's so bad.
I cannot help but stare,
At that face, so sad.
I step a little closer,
And see her wounded arms.
Though I try to comfort her,
She's suddenly alarmed.
As I reach out to touch her,
There's nothing there but air.
And the girl in front of me,
Has run away scared.
I understand; I withdraw,
Soon she reappears.
I wont push her now,
To face up to her fears.
Instead I will listen,
To her whispered woe,
And I sit here beside her,
As she bears her soul.
This girl sat next to me,
Is so terrified of the world;
She pulls her knees to her chest,
Into a ball she curls.
She's protecting her body,
From bad things she has known,
comforting her herself,
Though pain clearly shows.
Then this brave child before me,
Begins her sad tale,
And her face drains of colour,
She looks so worn and pale.
I can tell she is terrified,
Of the words she speaks,
for the first time she tells,
Of all the secrets she keeps.
This child, so beautiful,
Has been though such pain.
She carries the burden,
Like an old ball and chain.
She cannot forgive herself,
For another's wrongs.
It feels as if she's lost in time,
and will never belong.
I ache as I sit by her,
To hold onto her tight.
rock away the nightmares,
And to ease her plight.
But I fear if I touch her,
She will break apart.
This little girl suffers so,
With her wounded heart.
So all I can do for her,
As I sit here beside.
Is tell her I hear her,
And allow her to hide.
I hope that with time,
She will let me closer.
And not before time,
Her isolation is over.
Because I want to help her,
I hope that she knows.
I'm sorry I deserted her,
When she needed me most.
All the years have gone past,
And I ignored her tears.
I shut out her nightmares,
And ran from her fears.
But dear little girl,
I am starting to see,
That the fragile little child,
Is the you inside of me.
It is time I helped you,
acknowledged you are there.
And long overdue,
Let you know that I care,
Thank you, for surviving,
Though I ignored you so.
Thank you for fighting,
Though I buried you below.
But at last I am ready,
To at least set you free.
So fly away angel,
You're free to be me.

PRESENT
PAST

Warped and Twisted

Blows are flailed, hands are fisted;
Pummel down warped and twisted.
Violent pain and vicious fear,
Isn't that why I am here?
Can you see, the veil has lifted?
Just take a look: I'm warped and twisted.
Deadened soul, confused mind,
Journey forward but running blind.
Aching body, my feet are blistered:
The torment of the warped and twisted.
Wonder if I'll outrace my past abuse,
Wonder if for me, there's another use.
Call me back, my mind has drifted,
I can't control what's warped and twisted.
Thoughts are racing; heart is wild
Still that messed up little child.
But here I am, the pretence has shifted,
In truth you'll see I'm warped and twisted.
Now I am sure you'll turn away,
Leave me here another day.
How could I ask you to love; now the ash is sifted,
When all that's left is warped and twisted?

Caroline Roe

By Heather Williams

By Jillian Hotchkies

T e dre ed w ds

Allen

We're going to have to finish there
Those dreaded words
Does she sense my despair
Or only see me glare?

I haven't finished what I wanted to say
Please don't send me away-
Keep listening to me,
Let me sit here and be.

We're going to have to finish there;
Those dreaded words.
Would I ever dare
To cling tightly to my chair?

She glances over my shoulder
And mentally closes my folder
That's the end of my time
Go outside, pretend to be fine.

We're going to have to finish th
Those dreaded words
It just doesn't seem fair
Does she really care?

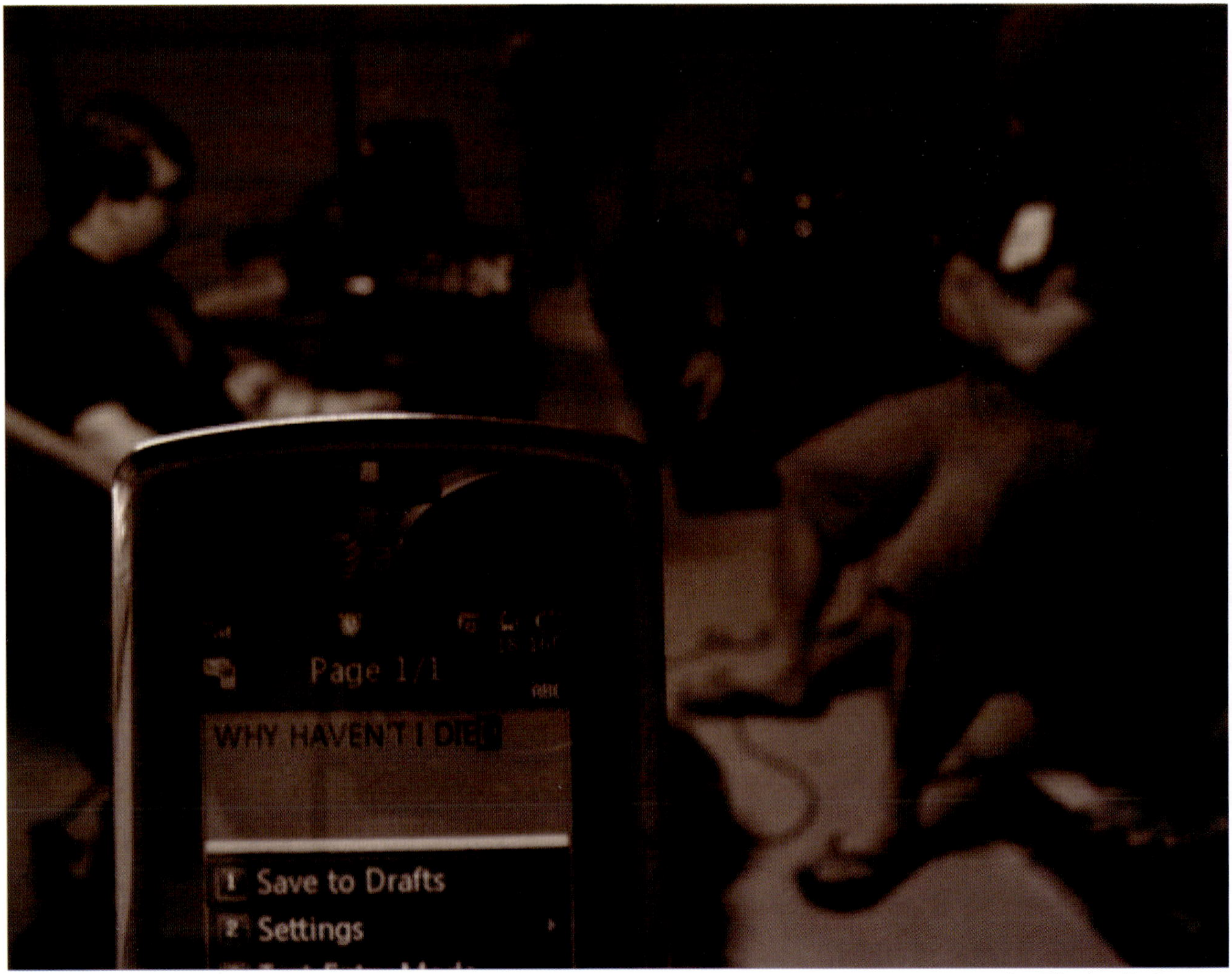

By Elizabeth Prasse

When I was asked to write something for this book it felt like an opportunity to share the experiences of working as a professional with young people who self harm. Whilst my background is in both General and Psychiatric Nursing, I have specialised in Child and Adolescent Mental Health (CAMH) and am a qualified Systemic Family Therapist. At the time of writing, my job entails working with young people and their families, both in a CAMHS Outpatient team and a CAMHS Self Harm Team. My role within the self harm team involves risk assessing young people who are admitted to hospital as a result of more serious self harming, whether it be an actual suicide attempt or not. Follow up care is then provided for both the young person and their guardians.

My plan is to share with you some of what my job entails, and both professional and personal work related reflections, which are influenced by the stories of those I feel privileged to have met through my work.

To begin, let me explain what actually happens when a young person is admitted to hospital and what you might expect.

Why are young people admitted to hospital following an episode of more severe self harm?

Admission is based on the recommendations by The Royal College of Psychiatry who state that all young people under 16, who are taken to hospital following an episode of self harm, are to be admitted to a Paediatric Ward. There will be occasions when the self harm requires hospitalisation for medical treatment and observation, but what about for those where this isn't the case? By admitting a young person gives the clear message that the self harming behaviour has been taken seriously. There is much evidence around to suggest that taking behaviour seriously is a crucial part of the healing process and can prevent repetition. If we think about ourselves at times of distress, most can remember the difference it can make if we felt our distress was taken seriously. Whilst being taken seriously may not in itself resolve actual difficulties, nevertheless, this can provide an important starting point.

A further reason for hospital admission is valuable thinking time that can be provided for the young person and their families/ friends, who are significant to the young person. It never ceases to amaze me how a bit of time out can take the heat out a situation. I have met young people and their carers on a ward when all are insistent they don't want to spend anymore time with the other.

Reassessing the situation a day later can make a real difference. Equally it can provide professionals time to reflect on more complex cases and come up with a plan, in some cases involving more than one agency to keep the young person safe and support families.

The young person will be seen in the Emergency Department and then admitted to a ward. As soon as the young person is considered medically fit, the Self harm team will be contacted. The young person and their carers will then be seen for a mental health risk assessment, to assess for risk of further self harm and suicide.

Now immediately by writing this I can hear the comments from any young person reading this 'but I am not mentally ill!' This can be a real concern, often voiced by the young person who fear their behaviour will be seen as an indication that they are 'mad' This is also often a fear of their carers who may struggle to make sense of the incident. It is worth a reminder here that self harm is a symptom; it is a behaviour and not an 'illness' in its own right. Nevertheless, we do know approximately 10% of people who present will have an underlying mental health difficulty, depression for example, and part of the after care role will be to provide support and treatment where necessary.

For the assessment the young person will be seen alone, initially and confidentiality explained. This can be very frustrating for guardians, who usually want to know why the self harm had taken place. At times there are things that the young person really wants to say but is afraid of how their guardian may respond. At other times there may be issues that we feel are crucial to share to keep the young person safe and part of our job is to help these concerns to be voiced.

The assessment involves asking a range of questions to the young person, for example: how are they coping in school? Has there been any bullying? What are their interests? How do they view themselves as a person? How is their mood and importantly, how has their mood been over the past couple of weeks? Their sleep? Eating? Are there any health factors that may affect the way they feel? How do they view themselves and those around them? Are there any family members who may be unwell either physically or mentally? Is there any history of drug or alcohol misuse?

The second part of the assessment goes into much more depth about the actual self harm. We are now looking at the risk element so we will ask questions like: is this the first self harming episode? What was actually taken, or done? Were they drinking or under the influence of drugs? What was the trigger factor? What was the intent? I.e. had they planned to kill themselves or was this an attention 'needing' act? (People often say it was 'attention seeking', but if you use the word 'needing' instead of 'seeking' it alters the whole perception).

Was the young person alone? Were they likely to be found? Had they written a note? What happened immediately after the incident? How do they feel on reflection, are they glad to have survived, are they likely to repeat? How hopeful do they feel about the future and what do they feel needs to happen to make a difference? These can be difficult questions to answer, but nevertheless responses range from "I will never do this again" to "as soon as I get out of here I am going to kill myself".

Guardians are then seen and their view of the incident listened to. Finally, together, we decide what support might be in place to prevent repetition.

On the basis of the assessment, decisions are made with the young person, their carers and hospital staff as to what happens next. Very rarely young people are admitted to a psychiatric in patient unit. The majority of young people are discharged home with a follow up appointment being given, ideally, within two weeks in the local CAMH service. Occasionally Social Services may become involved if there are concerns for the young person's safety. If Social Services are contacted the young person and carers will be informed, unless the young person's safety is put at serious risk.

It is important to take behaviour seriously, advice would always be that if you suspect that your child has seriously self harmed i.e. deep cutting, attempted strangulation, overdosing, please take your child to the Emergency Department, and if you aren't sure, then contact NHS Direct. If a young person has told someone they have self harmed and no action has been taken, there is a real likelihood that they will repeat in a more serious way.

On discharge from hospital, a follow up appointment will be offered, and in many instances only one appointment will be necessary. The shock can be the 'difference that makes the difference' and actually improve lives by opening channels of communication. So often I hear young people say "I didn't realise I could talk to my parents". From guardians how they have thought about life very differently. The simplest things that can make a difference; just sitting together watching the TV or playing a computer game together. Getting used to being in one another's presence, again, in a way that fits for you all.

What about those who won't talk? We do think about alternative ways to communicate and ideas that have worked are often very simple, like having a traffic light sign on the bedroom door, or encouraging the young person to write down their feelings. One young person I have known used to draw cartoons. It is a time to be creative, and also, possible to introduce some 'serious' fun.

Self harming and suicide attempts in young people can understandably cause much upset. Questions are often asked like 'why does a young person feel the need to attempt to take their own lives when they have everything to live for?' Maybe one way of making sense of this is to think of how we all develop coping strategies and problem solving techniques throughout life. So for example, the 15 year old girl who takes an overdose as a result of splitting up with her first serious boyfriend can be a devastating experience. As an adult it may seem an over reaction, but if we consider this might be the young person's first experience of a relationship breakdown (and remember our own experiences!) this can help.

Other commonly heard statements 'I just didn't realise they were so upset, they seemed fine to me' 'Why didn't they tell me?' Or 'I didn't realise they were self harming' It can be so hard not to self blame. Situations often happen with no warning, sometimes it is possible to look back and recognise changes that may have seemed insignificant at the time. A young person may have been communicating through their behaviour, they may have been spending much more time on their own, and less time with friends - they may have been more irritable or tearful.

What often clouds situations, as we all know, from our own experiences, other peoples experiences, and what we read or see via the media, is that adolescence is the most turbulent of times. It has to be! Developmentally this is the time when children are changing rapidly, both inside and out, and preparing to become independent adults in their own right. As a result it can be difficult to decide what is a typical adolescent reaction, or something to be more concerned about.

There are many reasons that could cause a young person to self harm. Bullying, with an increase in 'cyber' bullying. Struggles with studying, high expectations from others and self, abuse (all forms), worries about guardians health both mental and physical. Worries about parent's relationships, their own relationships, feeling different, isolated and cut off from others, issues around their sexuality, race, cultural differences, worries about their own health -there are so many reasons. Sometimes there is no obvious reason. Sometimes it can be a case of simply not realising help is available, or how to access the help.

Nevertheless, how do we manage self harm in our children? How do we get them to stop? How can we persuade the silent or loud young person to 'talk'? Through years of experience working with young people and their families, what I do know is telling anyone to stop a certain behaviour, getting angry, humiliating or bribing doesn't work!

You may find the following helpful. From a group run for young people who self harm a question asked 'What is the most helpful thing others can do for you?' maybe it might be worth seeing some views on what they considered doesn't help!

'Being asked why you attempt suicide – sometimes you don't know'
'People who don't listen properly'
'Those who say 'I know you are going to get through' '
'People who panic when you are upset'

And now- what does help

'Listen – don't advise'
'Be sensitive'
'Don't judge'
'Don't assume – ASK!'
'Deal with the feelings not the behaviour'
'Help me to think about alternatives'

Self harm in young people is an enormous subject and I feel I have only touched the surface in this writing. If I am to think of an overall message I would like to give, it would be to take your young person, and your own needs as a parent or carer, seriously. Don't be afraid, or ashamed, to seek support for yourself and your young person in order to help you stay strong.

Caroline Prance

Tomorrow will be better

William Soule

Photograph by Lorna Gillam

Today, before the alarm clock kookaburras,
I will get out of bed and make it. I will
fluff the pillows, tuck the sheets in neatly
and smooth out the wrinkles, open up
the window to watch the birds peck at worms.

Today, breakfast will not consist of custard-
filled donuts or black coffee sweetened
with Splenda. I will halve a grapefruit, bask
in the dawning sun with a cup of green tea,
count the morning glories and breathe.

Today, I will not shower. I will bathe
in chamomile and soak the afternoon away.
I will listen to the soft poetry of bubbles
bursting, trace my reflection with a finger,
white and wrinkled, as I watch myself drown.

Today, the television set will stay off,
the radio nothing but a mime stuck
in his box made visible. On the couch
I will prop myself up and read Dickinson
and enjoy the silence of being nobody.

Today, I will wait for night to envelope us.
A mollusk immures the discolored pearl
within its shell. I will dream of this desert,
this great basin, after the Great Salt Lake
inundates the sun. I will dream of oases.

Tomorrow, I will rise before the sun rises,
I will sing the songs of the early birds
before they sing, I will bloom before morning
glories flash their white petals to the light
like teeth, worms wet on the grass, alive.

Tomorrow, I will break a clam open, extract
the pearl, and hold it in my palm. Hold it tight.

Biography:

William Soule is a Filipino-American poet from Utah and is the editor-in-chief of the online literature and art magazine Clearfield Review. In his free time he serves as a literature gallery moderator for deviantArt, buys way too much organic food, smothers his pit bull with kisses, and obsesses over cookies.

Final Thought

I'll hold you.
I won't let you down.
I'm here.
It's all over.
You're not alone. Not anymore.

And you won't hear, won't listen or won't believe - but you'll know it.

And that's already a good beginning.